U.S. HISTORY 1820-1850

HISTORICAL TIMELINES FOR KIDS

AMERICAN HISTORIAN GUIDE FOR CHILDREN

5TH GRADE SOCIAL STUDIES

Speedy Publishing LLC

40 E. Main St. #1156

Newark, DE 19711

www.speedypublishing.com

Copyright 2017

In this book, we're going to talk about the history of the United States from 1820-1850. So, let's get right to it!

The end of the War of 1812 signaled a new era in American history. Although the United States had suffered many devastating defeats at the hands of British troops and their Canadian and Native American allies, including the destruction of the nation's capital, there had been victories for the Americans as well. The Americans had fended off the British in both New York and Baltimore.

WAR OF 1812

BATTLE OF NEW ORLEANS

They had also had a decisive victory at the Battle of New Orleans. After the war was over, Americans had a newfound feeling of patriotism and national pride. In many ways, Americans felt that they had won their battle for independence from the British a second time.

THE ERA OF GOOD FEELINGS

When James Monroe was elected president in 1816, it was the beginning of the collapse of the Federalist Party and the government was being run by just one party, the Democratic-Republican Party. It was a time when fighting between parties dissipated and there was a common mission to move forward to improve and strengthen the United States.

JAMES MONROE

The phrase the "Era of Good Feelings" was coined to describe this time period in history. The feeling of unification was so great that when Monroe ran for a second term in office, no one ran against him.

HENRY CLAY

THE AMERICAN SYSTEM

In addition to President James Monroe, another influential American during this time period was Henry Clay, a long-time statesman and orator who was Speaker of the House. It was Clay's goal that America should improve its infrastructure.

Clay was a brilliant man who realized that the United States could become a powerful and wealthy nation with a world-class transportation system. He also wanted

to see the work of American manufacturers protected and a strong United States banking system.

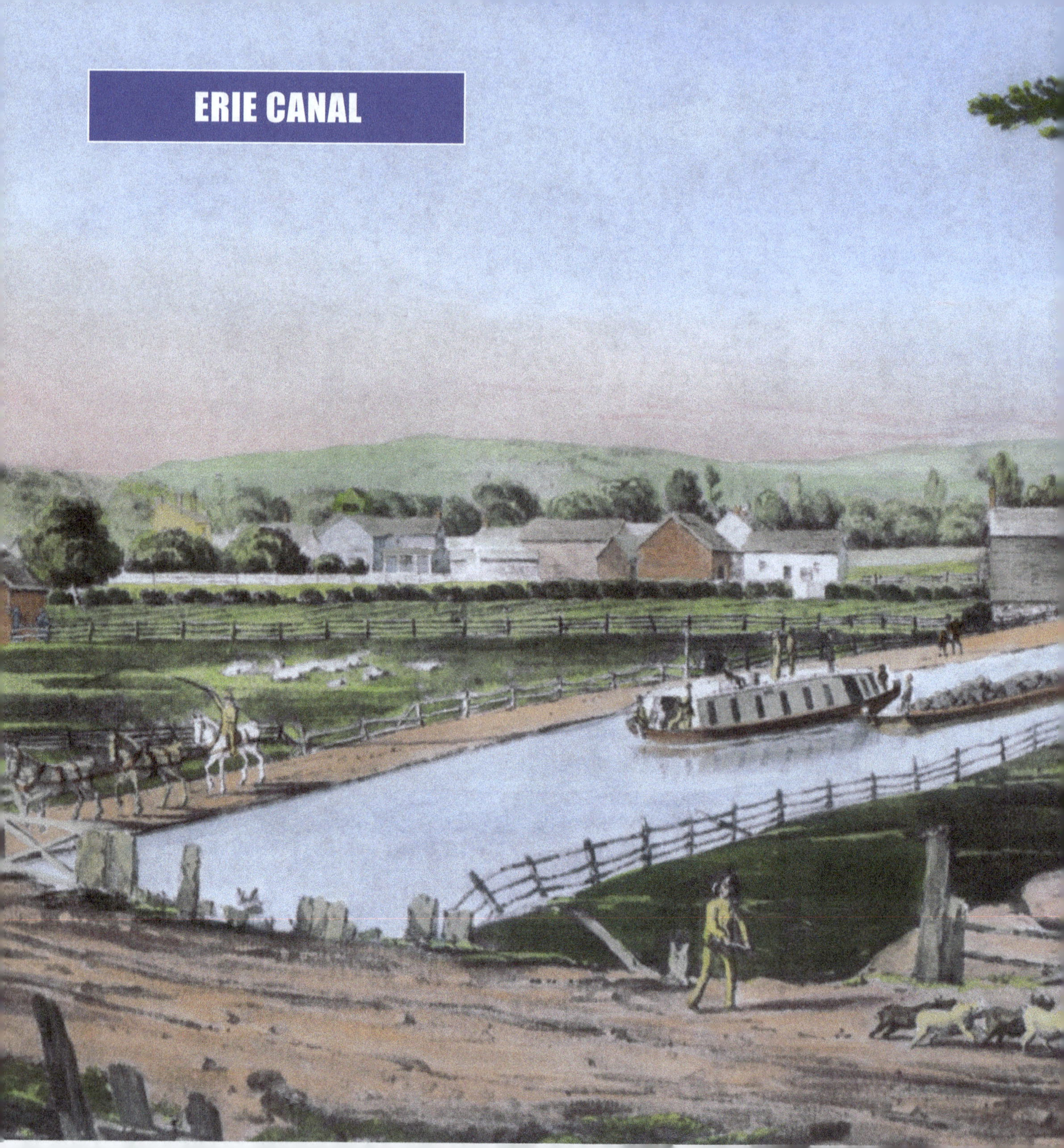
ERIE CANAL

To these ends, Clay pushed to link the West, with its farming strengths, to the North, with its industrialized factories. New canals, such as the important Erie Canal, and roads, such as the Cumberland Road, were built at Federal expense.

To protect American manufacturers so that consumers would buy their goods instead of goods from other countries, Clay persuaded Congress to approve the Tariff of

1816. Clay also pushed for a federal bank to be revived called the Bank of the United States.

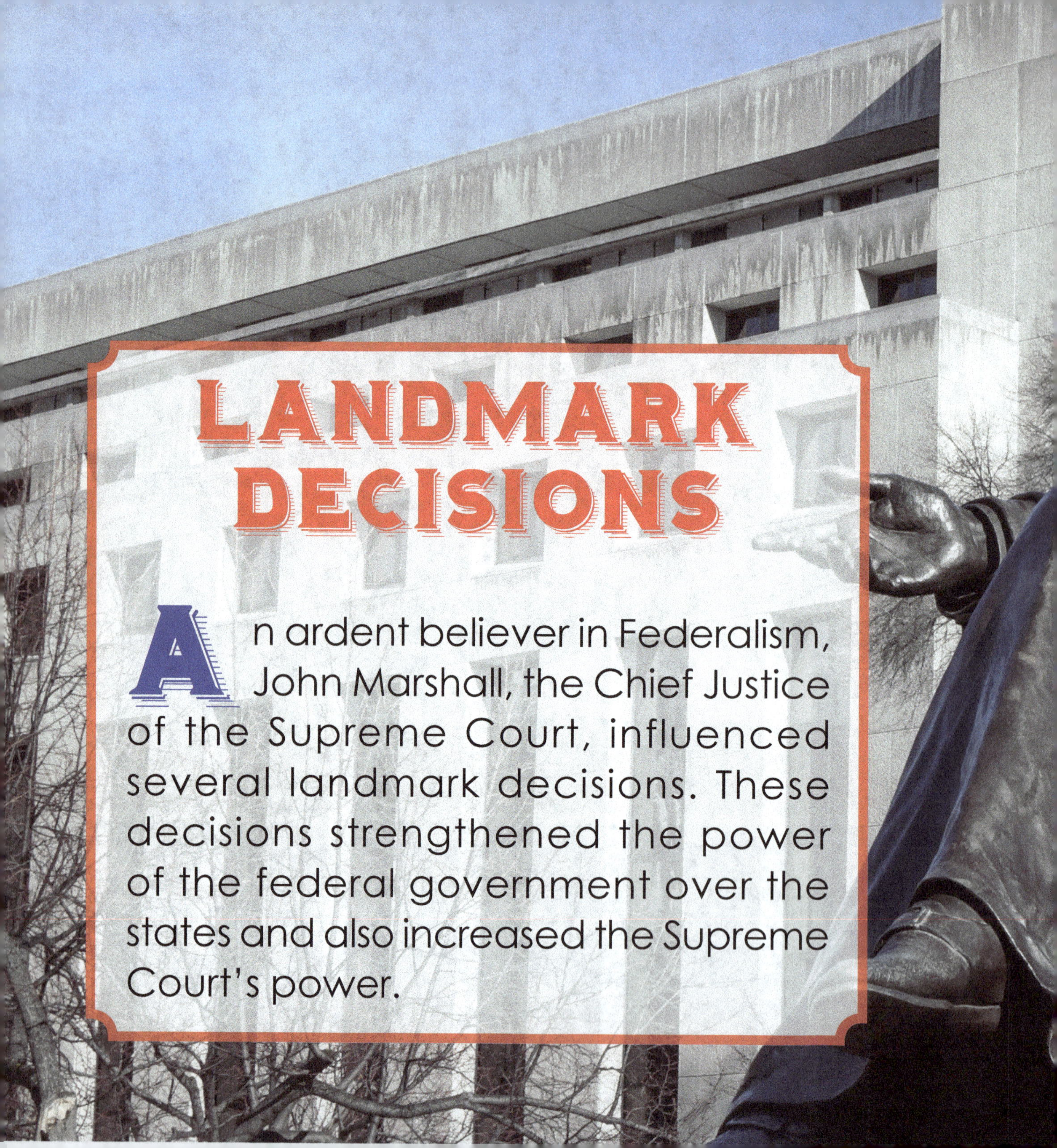

LANDMARK DECISIONS

An ardent believer in Federalism, John Marshall, the Chief Justice of the Supreme Court, influenced several landmark decisions. These decisions strengthened the power of the federal government over the states and also increased the Supreme Court's power.

JOHN MARSHALL

Some landmark cases were:

 McCulloch versus Maryland—The state of Maryland had tried to thwart a national bank in their state, but didn't win their case.

MARYLAND STATE HOUSE

DARTMOUTH COLLEGE

- Dartmouth College versus Woodward—
The court ruled that a national contract
couldn't be changed by state laws.

- Cohens versus Virginia—The court ruled that the federal courts have the right to review and pass jurisdiction over state laws when there's a question of Constitutional rights being violated.

WE MUST REMEMBER
THAT any OPPRESSION any INJUSTICE any HATRED
IS A WEDGE
DESIGNED To ATTACK OUR CIVILIZATION

FRANKLIN DELANO ROOSEVELT 1940

THE MONROE DOCTRINE

President James Monroe and John Quincy Adams, his Secretary of State, issued a statement in their message to Congress, which would later become known as the "Monroe Doctrine." It stated that the United States wouldn't accept any European intervention in the Western Hemisphere. This doctrine influenced American foreign policy from that time forward.

THE MISSOURI COMPROMISE

Unfortunately, the Era of Good Feelings didn't last long. There was an economic crisis called the "Panic of 1819" that caused a countrywide depression at the end of the first term of Monroe's presidency. Then, in 1819, Missouri applied for statehood. However, the Northerners didn't want Missouri admitted because they were a slave state. There was already sensitivity to the balance of anti-slave states and slave states.

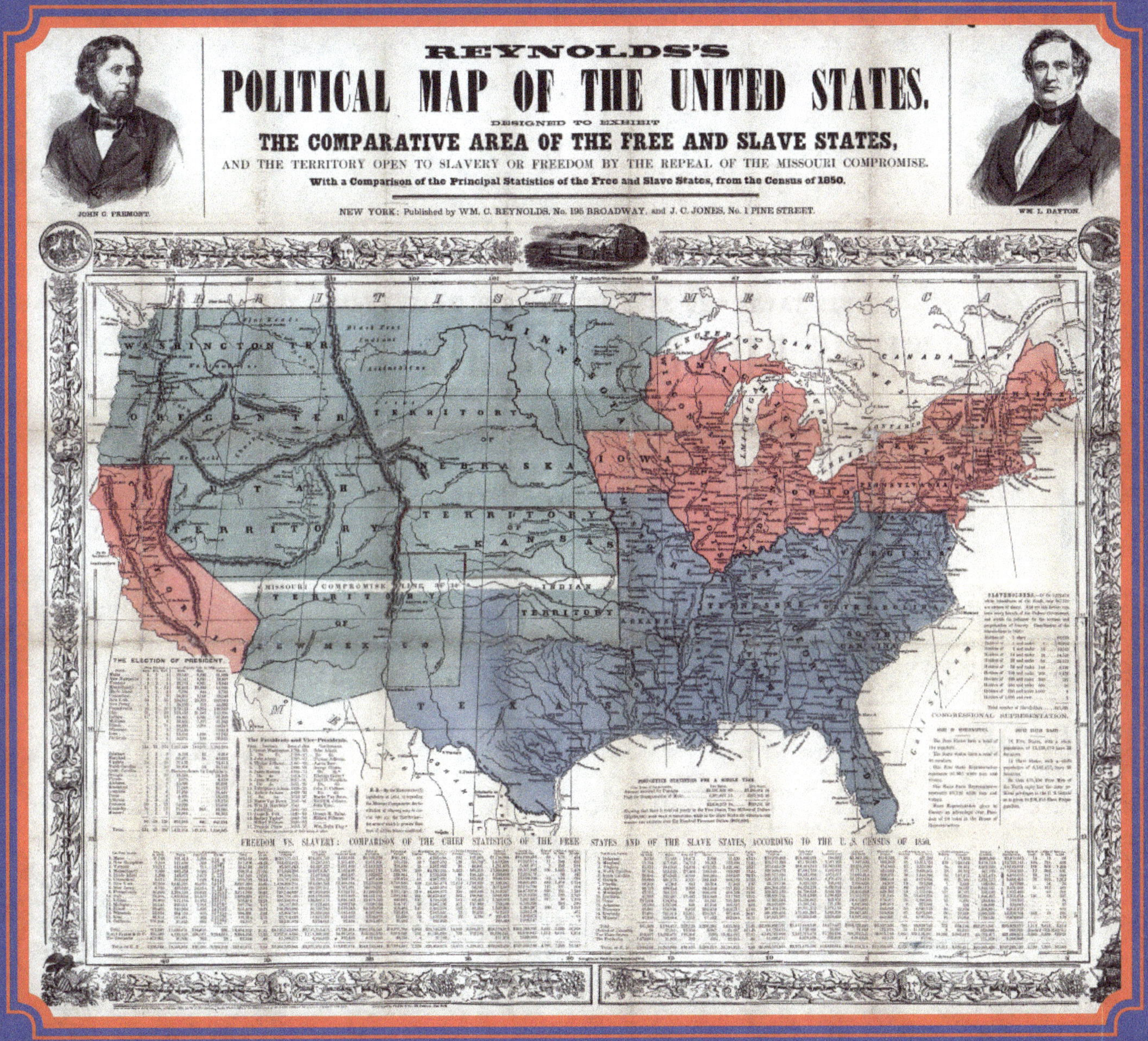
REYNOLDS'S
POLITICAL MAP OF THE UNITED STATES.
DESIGNED TO EXHIBIT
THE COMPARATIVE AREA OF THE FREE AND SLAVE STATES,
AND THE TERRITORY OPEN TO SLAVERY OR FREEDOM BY THE REPEAL OF THE MISSOURI COMPROMISE.
With a Comparison of the Principal Statistics of the Free and Slave States, from the Census of 1850.
JOHN C. FREMONT
NEW YORK: Published by WM. C. REYNOLDS, No. 195 BROADWAY, and J. C. JONES, No. 1 PINE STREET.
WM. L. DAYTON
THE ELECTION OF PRESIDENT
CONGRESSIONAL REPRESENTATION.
FREEDOM VS. SLAVERY: COMPARISON OF THE CHIEF STATISTICS OF THE FREE STATES AND OF THE SLAVE STATES, ACCORDING TO THE U. S. CENSUS OF 1850.

MAP OF FREE AND SLAVE STATES

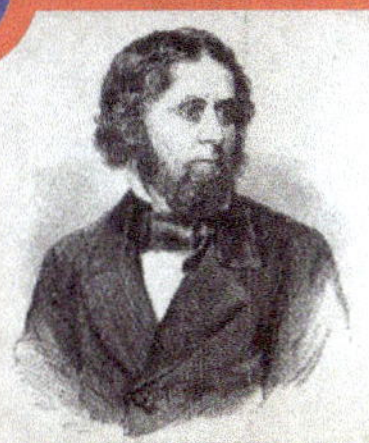

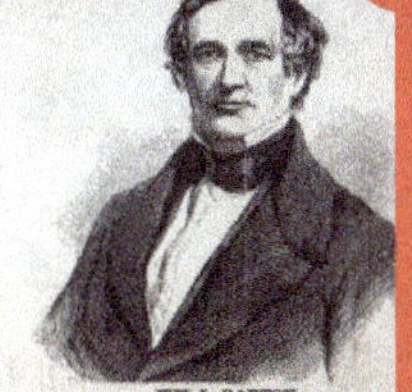

he Tallmadge Amendment was passed in 1819 to prevent more slaves from coming to Missouri. The southern states were very unhappy about the federal intrusion on their affairs. Henry Clay brokered a compromise. Missouri could be admitted as a slave state as long as Maine was admitted as a free state at the same time to maintain the balance.

THE CORRUPT BARGAIN

In 1824, the Era of Good Feeling ended with a competitive race for the presidency between John Quincy Adams and Andrew Jackson. Neither candidate garnered a sufficient quantity of electoral votes. Clay despised Jackson so he helped Adams who won and made Clay the new Secretary of State. The American people felt this political maneuver was a "corrupt bargain." Adams's reputation was forever damaged and his hands were tied during his four years in office.

JOHN QUINCY ADAMS

ANDREW JACKSON

ANDREW JACKSON BECOMES PRESIDENT

In the next presidential election in 1828, Andrew Jackson was voted as President. His two terms were filled with different types of crises. Northerners didn't like him, but southerners and westerners liked his rugged personality. At the end of Adams's term another tariff had been passed.

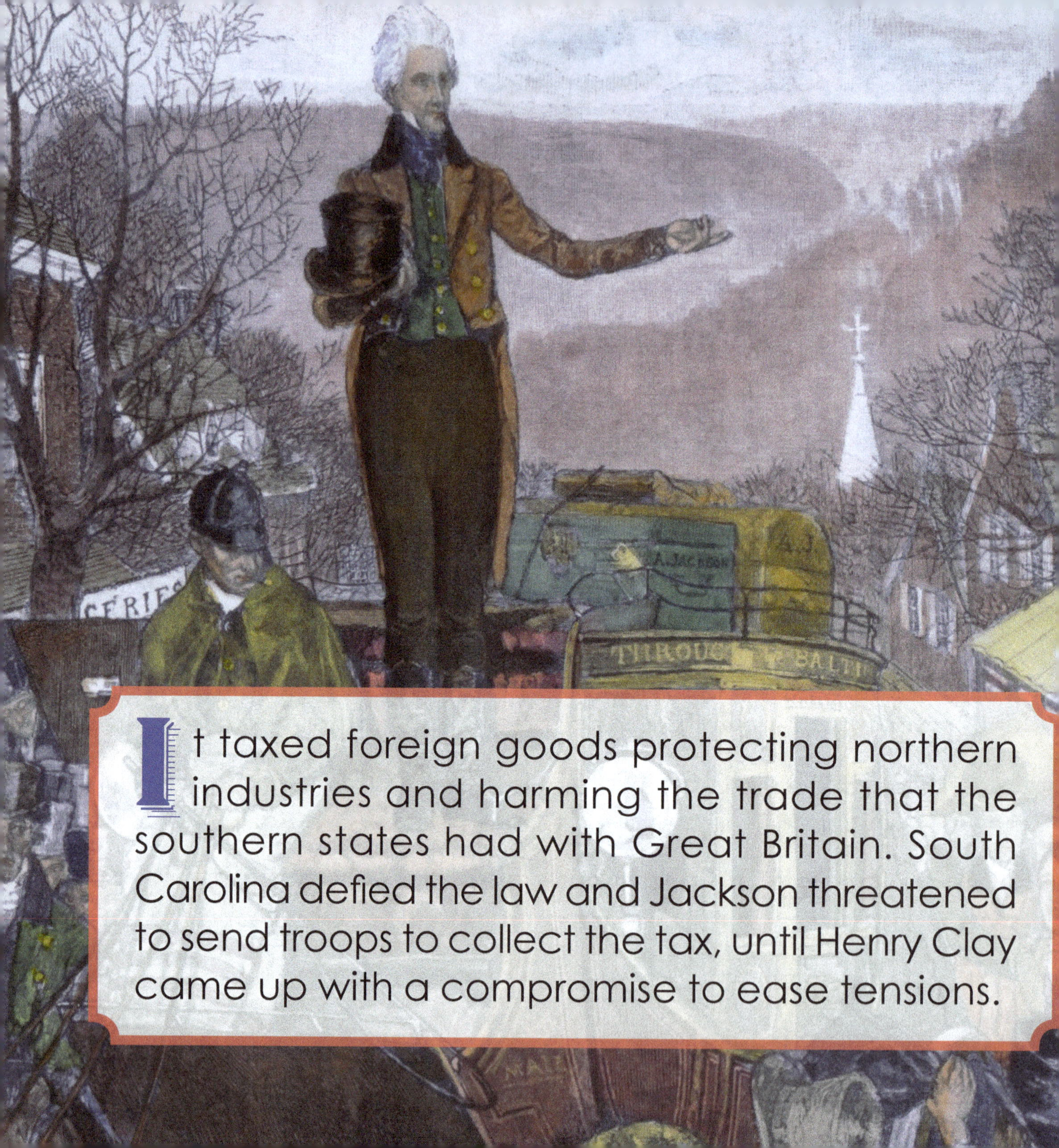

It taxed foreign goods protecting northern industries and harming the trade that the southern states had with Great Britain. South Carolina defied the law and Jackson threatened to send troops to collect the tax, until Henry Clay came up with a compromise to ease tensions.

THE RED EAGLE TAVERN
JNO. O'BRIAN
PROPR.
UNITED S
POST O
BAR ROOM
DRUG ST

THE INDIAN REMOVAL ACT

Jackson had fought against Native Americans during his military years. He influenced the passage of the Indian Removal Act in 1830. Over 100,000 Native Americans were moved to Nebraska and Oklahoma and many died on this "Trail of Tears."

uncommitted to any other course than the strict line of constitutional duty; and that the securities for this independence may be rendered as strong as the nature of power and the weakness of its possessor will admit, — I cannot too earnestly invite your attention to the propriety of promoting such an amendment of the constitution as will render him ineligible after one term of service.

It gives me pleasure to announce to Congress that the benevolent policy of the Government, steadily pursued for nearly thirty years in relation to the removal

THE UNITED STATES OF
FEDERAL
THE UNIT
THE UN
THIS NOTE IS LEGAL
FOR ALL DEBTS, PUBLIC
THIS NOTE IS LI
FOR ALL DEBTS, PU
THIS NOTE IS LEGAL TENDER
FOR ALL DEBTS, PUBLIC AND PRIVATE
G
CHICAGO
1
G₂
7
28237 G

JACKSON GOES TO WAR WITH THE FEDERAL BANK

Jackson didn't like the Bank of the United States because it was funded by a few wealthy individuals. In his mind it wasn't democratic. He didn't place any more federal money into the bank and deposited federal funds into smaller banks instead. This caused instability in the United States and brought on the "Panic of 1837." It also prompted Henry Clay and other important politicians to begin the Whig Party.

PRESIDENT VAN BUREN AND THE DEPRESSION

The next president, Martin Van Buren, inherited an economic mess. Without a strong federal bank, many smaller banks went out of business. Although Jackson had created the problem, many Americans blamed Van Buren and he lost the next election to William Henry Harrison of the Whig party. However, Harrison passed away a month into office and Vice President John Tyler took the office.

MARTIN VAN BUREN

JOHN TYLER

JOHN TYLER AND THE WHIGS

Henry Clay and the other politicians of the Whig Party were thrilled with Harrison's election, but when Tyler took office he didn't support their desire for higher tariffs, improved infrastructure, or a revived federal bank. Tyler's motivation for joining the Whigs was because he disliked Jackson. The Whigs were outraged and forced him to leave the party.

THE TEXAS CONTROVERSY

Southerners wanted Texas as a new slave state ever since the Texans declared themselves independent from Mexico in 1836. The Northerners didn't want more slave states so they blocked Texas from joining the Union.

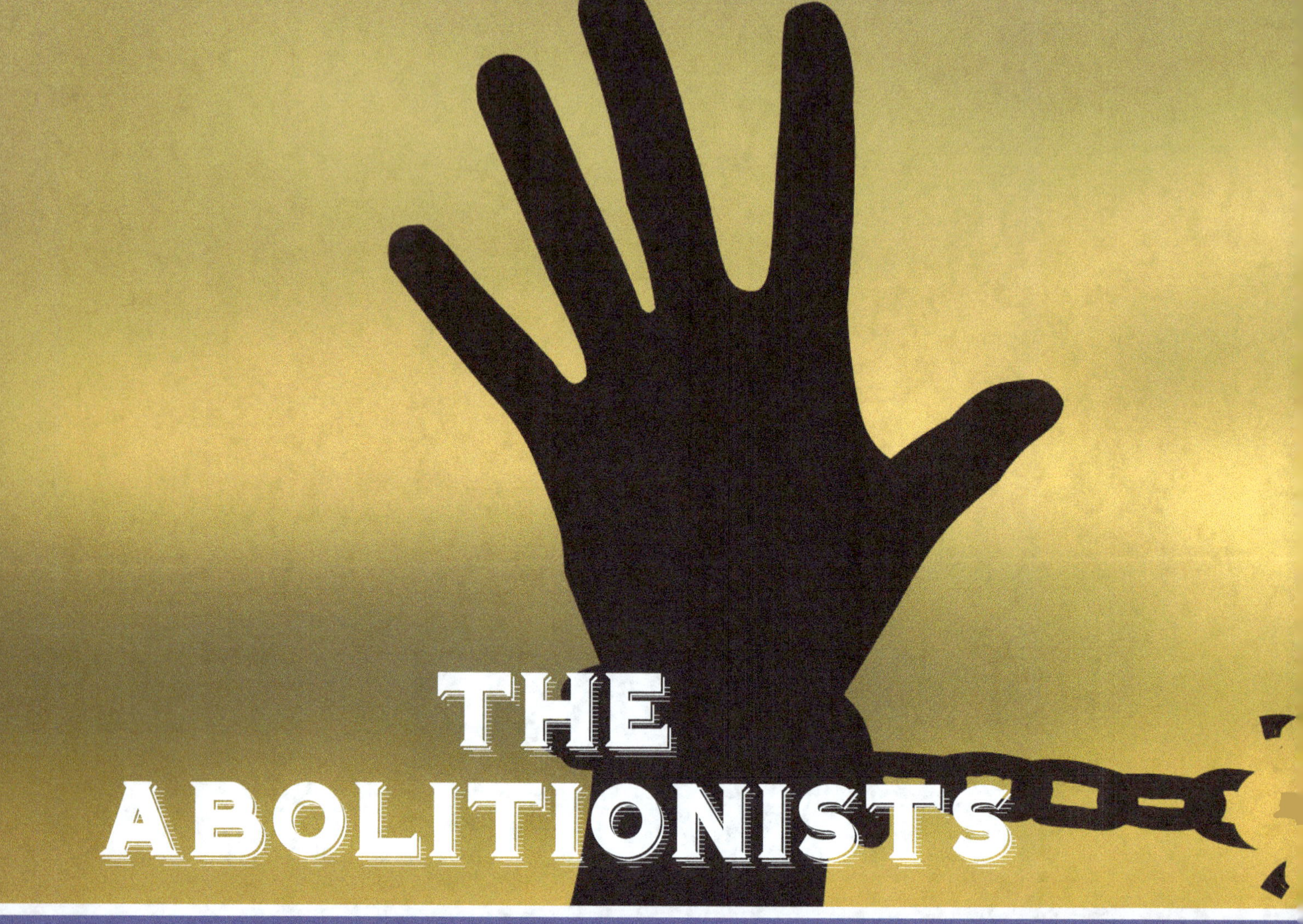

Those individuals who opposed slavery were called the abolitionists. They grew from a small segment of the population in the 1820s to a powerful group for social reform in the 1840s. Although they opposed slavery, they didn't yet take a stand for the equality of races. Only a few individuals,

such as William Lloyd Garrison, pushed for slaves being set free immediately. At the same time as this push for the abolishment of slavery, many women in the North started movements for women's rights as well as rights for those who were disabled. Hand in hand with these reforms there was a movement for new religious denominations.

THE MARKET REVOLUTION

From 1840 through 1850 and beyond, the United States economy was growing. The invention of the cotton gin had increased production of cotton in the South. The mechanical reaper had increased the production of wheat in the West. Ireland had a devastating famine after their potato crops became diseased and millions of immigrants had come to America seeking work in the Northern factories. German immigrants came in the millions too.

THE MEXICAN-AMERICAN WAR

President James K. Polk was elected in 1844. During his presidential term he greatly expanded the land owned by the United States by acquiring the Oregon Territory and igniting the

Mexican-American War, which the United States won. The United States was poised to expand its population and economy to the west coast.

TIMELINE EVENTS

1812—The War of 1812 begins.

1815—The War of 1812 ends.

1816—James Monroe is elected President ushering in one-party rule and the "Era of Good Feelings."

1816—The Tariff of 1816 is approved to protect American manufacturing.

1819—A financial crisis described as the "Panic of 1819" shakes consumer confidence. The economy suffers through 1821.

1819-1820—A crisis erupts when Missouri wants to join the United States as a slave state.

1819—The Tallmadge Amendment is passed to stop more slaves from entering the state of Missouri.

1821—Landmark Supreme Court case Cohens versus Virginia goes to trial.

1823—The Monroe Doctrine is issued, which warns European nations to stay out of American affairs.

1824—John Quincy Adams is elected President due to the support of Henry Clay and the American people see this as a "corrupt bargain."

1828—Andrew Jackson is elected President.

1830—The Indian Removal Act is passed and many Native Americans die on the journey to relocation.

1836—Texas declares itself independent from Mexico.

1837—Jackson kills the federal bank causing the "Panic of 1837."

1840—William Henry Harrison dies a month after taking the office of President.

1840-1850—Abolitionists who want slavery to end become a powerful force for change.

1840-1850—Millions of immigrants from the countries of Ireland and Germany come to America and are put to work in northern factories.

1844—James Polk is elected President and begins the Westward Expansion.

1848—The Mexican-American War comes to an end and America gains about 25% more land.

SUMMARY

The decades leading up to the Civil War was a time of great change in America. The early 1800s brought a new national spirit to the forefront and there was an "Era of Good Feelings." There was a push to abolish slavery and other social reforms for women's rights and the rights of the disabled. Economic instability eventually resolved itself as farming and industry thrived during the era of westward expansion.

Awesome! Now that you've read about the history between 1820-1850 before the Civil War of the United States, you may want to read about the Civil War in the Baby Professor book *The American Civil War - Blues, Greys, Yankees and Rebels. - History for Kids | Historical Timelines for Kids | 5th Grade Social Studies.*

Visit

BABY PROFESSOR
EDUCATION KIDS

www.BabyProfessorBooks.com
to download Free Baby Professor eBooks
and view our catalog of new and exciting
Children's Books